From Rob
5/0

CW01617441

Through the door

First published in 2014
by Poet in the City
Kings Place Music Foundation
90 York Way
London
N1 9AG

Design by Zoe Olaru

Printed in Great Britain by
Indigo Press Limited
Cambridge Road
Southampton
SO14 6TB

ISBN: 978-0-9930646-0-9

Contents

Foreword

Through the Door is an exciting and innovative collaborative project for Archives for London and Poet in the City. It enables the exploration of previously unimagined dimensions in archives and poetry, and opens both to new interactions and to new audiences of all ages. Archives and poetry are represented in various forms via *Through the Door*, including websites, short films, performance and poetry.

Archives for London (AfL) brings together everyone interested in archives in or about London – users, practitioners and enthusiasts. Through the passion, experience and expertise of our members and guests we help people get more out of the documents, photographs and films that make up our capital city's rich archival heritage. We support cross-domain and cross-sectorial initiatives and lead programmes specifically designed to improve access and engagement, knowledge and understanding of the London's unique documentary heritage.

In a similar way, Poet in the City regularly works with a diverse range of partner organisations to promote poetry to new audiences. Through its events, commissions, education and employability work, Poet in the City is challenging perceptions and putting poetry on a dynamic new platform.

It is the belief in their purposes, and the shared aims of outreach and broadening participation, that have enabled the creative work between Archives for London and Poet in the City to flourish in *Through the Door*. The recognition of the synergy in this particular cross sectoral engagement, and its value to the cultural life of London is evident in the generous funding support by Arts Council England.

Anne Barrett
Chairman, Archives for London

Introduction

In 2013 Poet in the City and Archives for London embarked on a poetry commissioning project to bring new audiences to poetry and archives. *Through the Door* was launched to highlight the opportunities for creatively engaging in local history.

The project commissioned six leading UK poets to uncover the hidden treasures of London's archives. From World War One letters at the British Library, to St Paul's Cathedral's Blitz damage and the diary of a grave robber at the Royal College of Surgeons, the poets have rediscovered some amazing human stories.

Sir Andrew Motion, David Harsent, Mario Petrucci, Fiona Sampson, Simon Jenner and Imtiaz Dharker are the six highly acclaimed poets featured in this book. The poets have been resident in a diverse range of London archives: the British Library, St Paul's Cathedral, the Freemasons, Hackney and Tower Hamlets, Imperial College and the Royal College of Surgeons.

The archives have opened their doors to a new type of creative investigation, offering up the historic details and footprints of a city, to be reimagined through poetry. Each archivist led the poet on a journey of discovery, and each poet took the journey in their own unique direction. From these fascinating hoards of material and information, the poets have identified details which open doors to some of the many stories to be told. The result is a treasure trove of contemporary poetry and a compelling insight into the richness of our past.

We hope that this collection encourages you to visit the archives and explore the stories inside, and provides insight into how poetry can shed new light on life and history.

Isobel Colchester
Chief Executive, Poet in the City

Imtiaz
Dharker
&
St Paul's
Cathedral
Archive

The Cathedral Poems

The Architectural Archive of St Paul's Cathedral contains material created by the Surveyor to the Fabric and by consultants, contractors, artists and designers, dating from c. 1850 to the present day. It documents the design, construction, decoration and maintenance of the fabric of the cathedral.

The records mainly stretch from the surveyorship of Francis Cranmer Penrose (1852 to 1897) to the present day. The Cathedral received two direct hits during the Blitz. The records reveal the extent of post-war reconstruction and redesign of the bomb-damaged east end, north transept and Chapter House. The main activity at the end of the 20th century was a twenty-year project to clean the interior and exterior of the Cathedral.

Sarah Radford
Archivist

Before I came to write these poems, what I really did in St Paul's was just eavesdrop. I was eavesdropping on the thoughts of the people who had written the notes, kept the logs, worked over the manuscripts, models and drawings that make up the vast archive of the cathedral. I was following clues about where they had had a new idea or changed their minds or been afraid, through their scribbles, erasures and alterations. What I was doing, really, was listening to the cathedral's memories.

The first meeting I had in St Paul's was in the cathedral library with its thousands of volumes in a magnificent galleried space that looks as if it still lives in the eighteenth century. The meeting was with the people who guided me into the archives, archivist Sarah Hale, librarian Jo Wisdom, Simon Carter who looks after the collections, and Canon Mark Oakley. Every door they opened for me led to many more, and I soon realised that it could take a lifetime to explore the treasures in this archive.

Before I could write anything at all, I had to overcome my awe of the place and the material.

It was then that the stories took over, telling themselves in clear voices out of John Donne's sermons, Christopher Wren's plans, the reports of the Surveyor of the Fabric or the wartime log books of the St Paul's Watch . Each story opened the way to many more, speaking of great events as well as quiet lives. My first set of poems circled around times of war, times when the city was under threat and St Paul's became a symbol of its spirit, the dome under constant attack but never destroyed by the bombs. One image that stopped me like a blow to the body was of a cherub cradled in the rubble, its chest dented. Looking at it, I thought 'It dents the heart'. That was the start of a sequence of poems and there are still many more to be written.

None of what I did would have been possible without a great archivist, Sarah Radford, who found answers to all my questions even when they went in odd directions. I hope this project will allow many more people, especially young people, to tap into the collective memory that is held in St Paul's and in all of London's archives. I hope they will feel the same sense that I do, of being part of a great story that belongs to all of us.

Imtiaz Dharker

Cherub, St Paul's

You were made to float in equal light,
at ease, your hands behind your head.
Swung high on praise in the sight of God,
you witnessed every prayer said, telling
your time by matins and by evensong, wild
bells ringing. You seemed, even cast in bronze
to have no weight, or only the weight of a child,
flesh rounded over birdlight bones.

Then the drone, the hush. The bomb
came looking for something to kill.
It never saw the Virgin, and glanced away
from the form of Christ, already crucified.
The one it chose as prey was you, at play,
wide open to its anger. With a fist of stone
the weight of a war came down on you.
Your ribs caved in where you took the blow.

Fallen, you are statue still.
This has not happened to a lump of metal,
but to a body that looks like a child's.

It dents the heart.

What are we to make of you?
A guardian, a bruised miracle, thrown
into the nave or on to today's front page,

the child who saved us,
the child we could have saved,
if we had been looking, if
we had been paying attention? In the aftermath,
the hesitant dust falls back to blanket you,
rubble tries to cradle you. Just
as we turn away, light seeks out your mouth
and wipes it with stained fingers. It takes the shine,

the refractions from your crumpled wound
and carries them up the columns
to rooftops that are waiting to be mended,
cratered streets and alleyways to be undented.
To the builders, the hammerers,
the crane operators and carpenters,
the engineers and makers,
it opens its fingers and offers

all it has to offer, the sigh
it took from you,
the lightness,
the stain of blue.

Unexploded

Like a giant boar, pig-ugly, it tore
out of the sky with its load

of death. Clumsy, it missed the mark
and snouted down into the road

snuffling the hem of the cathedral, too close,
too close. Unexploded, but eager to explode.

The saints held their breath, bells
bit their tongues, singing died.

Streets were emptied,
trams hushed, children sent away to hide.

The men dug their way to it,
pushing down to the monstrous thing inside,

wet cloth wound around their faces
against the murderous fumes, gases

let loose out of the city's punctured intestines.
Hours ticked by. Three days ticked by.

Three men down, twenty-seven feet in,
they worked around its lethal flanks.

Sapper Wylie and the squad
were gentle, gentler than midwives

when they brought it out, slick and slippery
as any newborn, the one-ton bomb.

Lieutenant Davies drove the beast,
its heart still ticking, across London,

past gaping houses, to the east.
There, in Hackney Marshes, at last

the creature's body was allowed to burst.
It blew a mirror image in the earth

of the thing it could not destroy,
a crater that might have been

the size of a cathedral, a crater
that could have taken the shape of a dome,

the scar of its intention overcome,
in time, with ragwort, cow parsley, burdock,

blurred by chaffinch and sparrowhawk,
an explosion of wings come home.

Exploded

On reading the sermons of John Donne

A prayer is said,
a story told. Under the dome
the Word explodes.

Channel of vision

The apostles have climbed up on the roof to look
at the world in black and white, the strut

of warehouses by the river, bridges, barges,
plundered cargo at the wharves.

Sunset burns the skyline down to size.
By sunrise it is back on its feet again

with billboards for Bovril,
Breakfasts Dinners Teas at Turner's,

the logos of banks climbing up Ludgate Hill.
The city draws its ambition on unused air,

and plots its future until
it stands there, concrete.

Clouds bunch together and mutter
darkly, threaten a riot

against barefaced glass,
the rise and rise that eats the sky.

Matthew, Mark, Luke, John, Paul
have seen it all: fortunes rise and fortunes fall.

Everything that lives will change.
Nothing is fixed except for the photograph

numbered and dated by the careful archivist.
Mist rubs out the horizon. It has no memory

of itself, or only the memory of an optimist.
Highbury and Islington swoop down to Smooth Fields,

scattering meadow flowers. Farringdon Street
turns itself back into the River Fleet.

The fragments are arranged
and rearranged

but for the watchers on the roof
there is no impediment,

no then or there or here.
The sightline is clear.

First light slides over the curve of the earth
to illuminate a world that is always unfinished,

life on the verge of becoming,
the word still forming.

Ringing the changes

Twelve bells were donated to St Paul's,
many by the Livery Companies of London

The market has lost its sound track,
no vans from Scotland or Wales unloading
their stock, hooks swinging, doors slamming,
shutters banged back. All the usual effing

and blinding has stopped for the day. A walk away,
twelve bells have found tongues. The clapper strikes
for the Company of Drapers, treble as hangers
on rails, flicking a tail to the Fishmongers
in a shiver of scales. The Grocers sing out
on a note you could eat, seasoned by Salters.
Clothworkers shuttle it on to the Taylors
over six days of toil, singing looms, oinking pigs,
lowing cattle. The ring goes full circle from treble
to tenor, tenor to treble, all the world's trouble
turned around on a peal of pure sound.

The tower is alive with it, the air vibrates
with the thrust and the weight
of bells being swung, the changes rung
from the top of St Paul's.

The city's business becomes
a calling of bells.

The Fabrick

Look up at the vast span of the drum,
the lantern's height, the dome.
See how the architect lifted the weight
of all this magnificence away

from foundations laid on uneasy clay,
the shifting earth, the splitting skin,
the frailty of rubble at the core.
Be aware the fabrick will decay.

Take ye away the stone.

Lift from the heart the weight.
Bring to light the hidden face.
Find, inside the resonating space,
the way to live, the living poem.

David Harsent
&
The Library
and Museum of
Freemasonry

Six Masonic Sonnets and a Hewn Stone

The first lodge of freemasons in the world was founded in 1717 in London. The archive collection includes records of the United Grand Lodge and Supreme Grand Chapter of England, their predecessor bodies, buildings and sites associated with Freemasonry, charitable bodies associated with Freemasonry, and individual Freemasons.

The archives include resources for studying the history of freemasonry in England, Wales and across the globe from Australia to Zambia.

Treasures in the archives that reflect this inclusivity include several letters from an eighteenth century black freemason, Prince Hall, of African Lodge in Boston, America and a loyal address from the son of the Nawab of the Carnatic. Other documents reveal details about Masonic membership among members of the Sikh, Zoroastrian and other communities in England and south-east Asia.

Susan Snell
Archivist and Records Manager

1717
1967

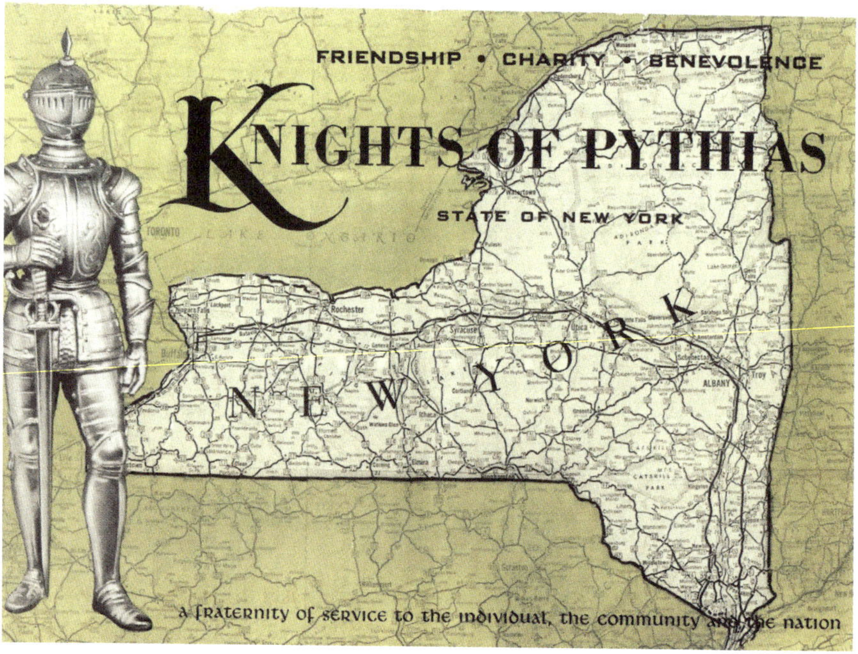
FRIENDSHIP • CHARITY • BENEVOLENCE
KNIGHTS OF PYTHIAS
STATE OF NEW YORK
NEW YORK
Rochester
Syracuse
ALBANY
a fraternity of service to the individual, the community and the nation

It was Susan Snell – the archivist at the United Grand Lodge of England (Freemasons Hall) – who gave me the first hint of how I might get a sequence of poems out of the wealth of material she made available to me. She made mention of Loveless (or Lovelace) Overton, clearly a Freemason of great interest to her: in fact it was evident that she had grown fond of Loveless over a distance of nearly two centuries, and that fondness was both intriguing and affecting. It showed me how close and dedicated an archivist can be to what lies in her care.

I decided to write about Loveless, not least because his story was fascinating for seeming unique (he was black, illiterate, and a bugler in the King's Royal Dragoons when he became a Freemason in 1805) and in making that decision, I came to see that I might produce a sequence where each poem featured a famous Mason with a particular story to tell. Those available to me were an impressive, diverse and surprising bunch: Annie Besant, Laurel and Hardy, Oscar Wilde, Louis Armstrong, Kipling, Mozart, George Gershwin, Casanova…

The sonnet is not a form I've much used, but it offered opportunities to ring the changes in ways that seemed appropriate to subject. The girls from the Ruspini school drew mono-half-rhyme to match the vigour of their questioning; Annie Besant's monologue found both internal rhyme and end-line rhyme, which gave her voice a sad insistence; Louis Armstrong's sonnet has three strong caesuras in each line, a hard internal rhyme, and a rhythmic beat that echoes that of Storyville jazz. And so on, with varied compositional methods for each of the six sonnets and their subjects. I also saw a way to incorporate, in the title of each poem, an appropriate Masonic attribute or symbol.

The sequence ends with a shape poem which gives a deliberately oblique account of Freemasonry while also instancing one of the most crucial of Masonic symbols – a hewn stone, the ashlar – that represents the hope of virtue through instruction.

David Harsent

Girls from Ruspini House debate the attributes of a supreme being

Harriet Ann Vernet (deemed 'a proper object'): 'Then if God
is all-powerful but evil still exists God isn't good,
but if evil does exist and God would ban the bad
then God is not all-powerful.' Mary Ann Ruscoe: 'They said
I should be sent home, there was corruption in the blood.
If I was born in sin, and that was meant, how could
I change?' Frances Sansum, then: 'You know I prayed
to come here, though known to be infirm. It was allowed;
should I thank God for that?' Ann Kane: 'You should.'
Ann Martin: 'I think God is among us, though his tread
falls light on the ground.' Sophia Kewney: 'I was made
to believe, to say I believed, and then somehow I did.'
Sibella Proctor ('a *very* proper object'): 'All that I've read
on this leads me to suppose God lives but loves the dead.'

Annie Besant considers a skull: Memento Mori in the chamber of reflection

Either the mystery has gone from this, or this
is the mystery: the human shape beneath the shape
by which we know each other. I faced my father's face
on his deathbed and saw hope beyond hope
that only mystery could replace, coming soon in place
of who he used to be. I watched him change, and change
back again. Next day my mother's hair was white-on-white...

I'm held in this blank stare, that hollow look the look
my daughter gave me when they took her from me, took
what was usual and rich and turned it strange, estranged
and lost to me as I was lost to her as God was lost
to both of us. I hold this head and hold this head to be
what once held Kabbalah, Hermetica, at least the least –
once here, now gone – of what it is we know we cannot know.

Louis Armstrong's cake-walk on the chequered pavement

Claims he was born | Fourth of July | underneath | a clear blue sky
Red light district | New Orleans | life barely worth | a hill of beans
One step forward | one step back | sometimes the white | sometimes the black
Music perhaps | or else the sound | of gunfire from | the 'battleground'
His daddy soon | walks out the door | leaves them flat | and leaves them poor
Streetwise Louis | takes daddy's role | stealing food | or hauling coal
His mother takes | another tack | and makes her living | on her back
One step on | one to the side | the squares depict | the Great Divide
The Home for Coloured | Waifs and Strays | is where he lives | and where he plays
Buys a cornet | buys a suit | gets married to | a prostitute
Riverboats | King Oliver | the band is good | but he's the draw
All to gain | nothing to lose | Heebie Jeebies | West End Blues
Even though | he's made his name | money, possessions, | world-wide fame
No one knows | what Louis lacks. | Step on the squares | avoid the cracks.

Compass and square: graffito carved by Oscar Wilde on his prison wall

I didn't kiss him; he wasn't pretty enough.
Or something much like that.
And a sudden silence in court; and no way else to bluff.
He stood on the platform at Clapham Junction, handcuffed, while they spat
and jeered. Nothing of wit to be had; nothing off the cuff.
Our very dress makes us grotesque. We are
the zanies of sorrow.
How would you make the best of this? How would you try to square
the circle? You might lie awake as a mythical tomorrow
shrinks to symptoms of love; you might
see out the night
exhausted and cold to the bone
cutting this image into the wall, adding below:
Pain unlike pleasure wears no mask, symbol and words both set in stone.

Lovelace Overton under the all-seeing eye

Loveless by a slip of the pen or Loveless by design;
to be found bottom-left and smiling among the trunks,
the hay-cart, the 'sweethearts', babies, wives, (and one
bird-cage) in Henry Perlee Parker's overloaded canvas
Baggage Wagon of the King's Dragoons; Loveless
because lacking love, or else Loveless in truth
if Loveless was your given name and Lovelace the corruption;
Loveless '...thirty eight years of age, illiterate, six feet
in height, hair black, eyes black, complexion black,' a trumpeter,
his discharge citing 'shortness of breath'; Loveless
self-styled, maybe, but never the bitter joke
of someone with no love to give; Loveless who kept
'a tung of good reporte'. Loveless, I think the best of you.
I pick you out of history and offer you a handclasp.

A gathering at the United Grand Lodge of England

'A woman is only a woman, but a good cigar is a smoke':
Kipling to George Washington, who only half-smiles at the joke.

Mozart and Schikaneder take time out to dispute
Papageno's entrance, Act One, The Magic Flute.

Laurel tells Hardy the story of the broken-hearted clown.
Hardy tells Laurel the story of the straight-man's nervous breakdown.

George Gershwin's eyes are closed: something's coming through
Which could be a fantasy in black or Rhapsody in Blue.

Peter Sellers and Michael Caine discuss
Which will be next to come along: a girl or a London bus.

Marc Chagall and Goethe, Voltaire and Mendelssohn
Lorca, Burns and Conan Doyle all stand beneath the sun.

Hogarth and Casanova exchange some anecdotes
On matters somewhat lickerish, while Susan Snell takes notes.

Masonic Square

A HANDCLASP A KISS AN EAR SMITTEN OFF THE ASHLAR FIRST UNHEWN THEN PERFECT WHATEVER IS HIDDEN THE GHOST IN THE MACHINE BLAKE'S URIZEN GREAT GEOMETER KNEELING TO ENCOMPASS THE WORLD THE FORTY-SEVENTH PROPOSITION OF EUCLID OTHERWISE THREE-FOUR-FIVE AND SO AT THE DEAD CENTRE OF THAT STONE • A BLIND EYE AND YOU MUST YOURSELF BE BLIND IT IS SAID BEFORE YOU CAN SEE WHAT IS THERE TO BE SEEN WHICH IS WHAT MIGHT BE CO-OPTED AND TRADUCED ALL THIS DETERMINED ON THE FEAST DAY OF JOHN THE BAPTIST AT THE GOOSE AND GRIDIRON SO CALLED IN THE CHURCHYARD OF ST. PAUL'S BY BROKEN COLUMNS THERE AND SO MOTE IT BE

Simon
Jenner
&
Hackney
Archives

Out of Asyla

Hackney Archives cares for the archives and local studies collections of the London Borough of Hackney and makes them available to the public for research. Our holdings include published works on the history of Hackney and East London, printed ephemera, paintings, prints and photographs, manuscripts, local newspapers, and maps.

In addition to the official local government records, we hold the records of a range of businesses, many voluntary organisations including political associations, trade unions, welfare charities and societies. We hold some records of prominent local families and many local churches. The oldest document in our collection dates to 1356.

Libby Adams
Principle Archivist

Elizabeth Green
Access and Outreach Officer

JAMES LIBRARY
Hackney

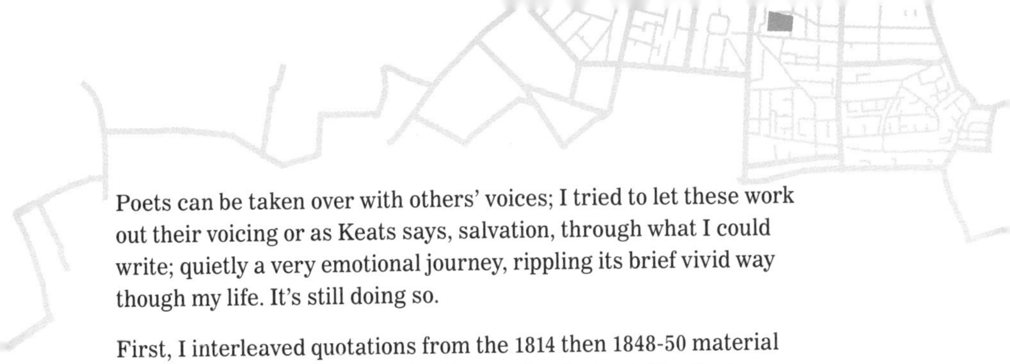

Poets can be taken over with others' voices; I tried to let these work out their voicing or as Keats says, salvation, through what I could write; quietly a very emotional journey, rippling its brief vivid way though my life. It's still doing so.

First, I interleaved quotations from the 1814 then 1848-50 material then riffed this with the imagined narrative derived. The first poem emerged from a set of resolutions. The next moved along the same process; I added here just one fleck of fiction. A virid third sketched anaphoric lines later interleaved with cholera - a reverse process.

There was an intuitive settling-in of material, then poems, till they clicked. I was surprised, pleased. The gamut's from rhyme royal to modernist/antiphonal, allowing information to breathe and lift.

I expanded with four poems formally rhymed with absorbed narratives via ledger notes in compulsory HB. I was keen to honour all I had, names, depositions, scratches of feeling I'd extrapolated - with a fictional inference. Some throw up the livid voice-catch of injustice, abandonment, emigration or more subtly ermine charity disguising other abuses.

Sometimes the Board's humanity as well as its officialdom, I hope, shines out. One poem's a stock/pea-soup recipe, interleaved 'to taste Mondays mouths'. As with all information it's as accurate as possible. A poetry version of verbatim theatre, almost. I've quoted verbatim, allowing period rhythms to direct sensibility, colour tone, sonance. To flesh characters through flickers of harrowed depositions.

These later poems are slightly lighter in texture. Finally I returned to a poem I wrote in January knowing just the refuge's outline. This poem now found itself filleted in a reverse freighting with émigré particulars. I then revised the others.

I might write more outwith this project. Some young women proving fiercely articulate despite Victorian filters, I took license to evoke a private language, set of intimacies that occurred in such society. It's ultimately intrusive, but I hope honours these resonant voices. A privilege I took seriously: to be true to their unquiet spirit, often their burning letter.

Simon Jenner

23rd July 1814

Resolved: Coutts, Charteris, deposited sums of credit
for investing –
    for infesting us with the hem of your debt.
Inattentions of Angela on the Sabbath –
    this calico day I'll jar soot out of clouds,
    now all's safe from Boney's drift of war.
    If he'd won what then – what smock colours
    could we have run up - what liberties beat out?
Resolved: Eleanor Gordon discharged with credit to seek credit
    sweet goody Gordon lets who will to spend it.
    Thomas cooped in Chatham Dock, typhoid breaks fleets, wins
    hands over in Dalston – *were you minding the sermon?*
    Minding my merman, ma'am.
Resolved: Sylvia Cox, Sarah Edwards recommence service
    Minding minding - thankfulness – for typhoid, for Hackney?
    Twopence to salt your tongue on brass
    on a Monday burnishing.
Resolved: Mrs Clark strike her daughter home.
    Sissy Clark was a spark; where's she soused now?
Resolved: Chaplain one hundred thirty five pounds credit
    for the lining of leaden souls.
of Sarah Gibbons drummed out for wicked ma and pa
decline to take her -
    from her miasma of the fleet.
    discharge her to the one profession – I heard them –
    thirteen – with whoring orders from her mother
    fall to servicing the fleet, fleet to childbed fever.
Resolved -

13th May 1848

Angelica Williams, fifteen, stole from befriending mistress;
Suffolk, St Newell. - Not a suitable case.
    No-one in St Newell dare ask why I did.
Ann Faulkner Presented Rev Hambledon,
fathers labours/cannot settle.
Mother deposes 'only victuals and it's those
vicious idle girls'. Not a –suit...
Frances Cranston so sadly depraved – wishes to reform,
cannot as she is – other workhouse girls
for years prized her fingersmithing.
Parents brought her up to thieving
Admit her if the Shoreditch Rev will have her back.
    That's his sure-ditch hope.
Alice Faulkner; stole Japanoiserie –
claims to speak the bowl's tongue.
Chaplain claims he caught strange gutturals off her
one free half Saturday; the girl invented –
    intricate chase-strokes brushed out of porcelain.
Ann says she's none of theirs – a changeling foisted brat.
Commit to Bedlam....
15th May: Fled with five pounds to France;
reported entourage of Princess de Polignac as – ?
interpreter.

16th June 1850: Cholera

Rudd the gardener to apply for enlargement -
    death takes six feet, adds six inches -
from Mr Turner, not the secretary;
    death fixes the glass cabinets to front repute
admonished, via the chaplain five shillings, six months;
    death tries a new language
the sewage ditch, replaced with a four inch pipe
    death writes white on black
draughtsmen cover nuisances with our clay
    death is lost in translation
baked from the wheel, knurled each lip
    death is a farting dancer, lost control
drunk into the unsanitary ditch mouth,
    death is an albino by the cemetery, whiting us out
slobbering feverfew at the herb garden
    death on a lead, snapping rabid at heels
tripped headlong to stench-purge fennel,
    grief is time out backwards
figwort root shits the queen's evils, for thyme;
    grief's the anaphora, death the rhyme.

27th November 1850:
Eliza Lambert Admitted

Unthread the light round Master Lane,
his leather halo, let me have it all
twist with the mahogany stitch-awl;
my fingers round his throat again.

He took my devil part with his angel share
unhemmed the theft of dress and violet shawl
represented my fall
thirteen and a half, half Newgate years

half dead father, dead mother, half
his – curdled white and small
whey crudded for the way – he – tall
stooped – touched – his soft laugh

touched me better than others
when dry of me, when I shudder, pall
in games began to sour and gall
when mistress scold and master smothers,

he ravelled me pearl, plain words -
Newgate - deaths, the evil caul
of whoring born over me, he'll scrawl
and scratch his conscience out like turds.

17th November 1849

Mondays, pea soup Saturday's salt pork liquor
being two pounds penny pepper – salt onions carrot suits
leek to taste – salt two ounces suet dripping four ounce flour
one third pound Patna rice – boiled fifteen minutes

thirty three pints, mouths to flicker
thin lives to the tallow of candle flame, flute
hunger, needle, earth closet, needle, hunger
salt, to taste to taste Mondays mouths to mute

4th November 1848: The Submission

So, British Ladies – we're three – by strapping –
don't ask - young women – scrimped by dint – don't ask
the *William Walden* – bound for Perth;
two of us twins, the third, the Refuge knows me bright-

needling my days to bone nineteen – tempting –
the bluey west coast answers with its life mask:
marriage, children run fast bleached into salt earth.
Two of us fared: the third's hand stretches calloused – white -

12th October 1848: Deposition

The board reminds the government –
lopping the third thousand off their grant
loses us all that sum of good they meant;

casts off those buoyed in the men's refuge: grant
to ministers niggard of scale, lank
in mildew double-entries, rationales to slant

our fifteen pounds per annum stank
to their nineteen-four at Newgate.
Their greater outlay's schooled to rank

thieving skilled to a flying loom's rate
punishing whose yarn? We are lent
lives, this ledger's cut, lives; on this date -

24th November 1849: Frances Reeves *Too Bookish*

Pacefully; Alice minted us a word
not in her Johnson, lit a raspy dry spill,
roar up this snug, Saturdays, as days fill -
like waterlogged footprints the seconds blurred.

So I tag November's soggy arrows round
chervil long plucked; Alice's hair they tried
snatch last spring as she bit and straight off flied
next minute, her singular words without sound

erased, save from the register of our crumbled spine
I secrete here: *pacefully, gruellish; chossy* nights;
chossy nights, Alice, your future brights
new senses with a touch no longer mine.

So slip me this *pacefully* filched from our hours
whilst Boards equivocate and blanch my worth:
honest, plain, a flat thing printed for the earth
I can just breathe through whatever throbs as ours.

Introit: Northern Visitor, Southern Ends: 10th October 1848

You from the north where they don't vote?
Don't try weaving us out.
Elizabeth Cooper: too wild, words are her
misconduct; send to her father.
We're not loom-snapped somewhere in your archival room.
Don't breathe us through your flax dust of Halifax
or what you imagine flax is, arrowed south here.
There's no-one called Penelope
who'll unravel promised stories every night.
Rough learning turned to raillery against -
That's you, that's you, that's you.

Dr Lang, applied for the second twin to Adelaide
again on the *William Walden.*

My raft's slipped every friend over the side
every woman but me, clutching my
slow dream hands.
Eliza White, sufficient confidence to
recommend to service – Dr Lang suggests -
When I woke they
clutched me, in the sick bay, before
we sewed them in sail-shroud.
Will the Refuge pay the difference?

Love's stranded between hemp and lace.
What you're born, burn with, won't wash out –
my brief sweet body won't whiten, so for him
I cut some lace and they cuffed me.
A screw of salt and they –
After, they said it's that I had a whore's face.

So he found a shining shy one of fourteen;
no browning, no tannery time had she.
Another refuge brat like me, but *delicate* -

Mary Swan turns too ill if she stays with her aunt
Accepted at 2/6.
    So nothing but Hackney's free air, when I stepped
    still stung to be living – yeast frothed
    out of that cell's dead ferment. I wasn't of it –
    not it nor boned any curvy place out of it;
Mary Swan released for 2/6 surety -
    he'd gone to white-neck, child white arms months ago.
    Convicts' bones are white as any queen's;
    they glitter here to Australia, singing
    new starts to death or a crack at living.
    What ricket man, what runty litter should I gust
    before the yellow fever gets me? Was Hackney worse?
    Are you still boxing their gold-rimmed ears,
    Liz Cooper, like those who threw you back?
    A hand held dying you knew from a child's;
    let the body snatchers hold you dead.

    Lizzie, we're glints in Mr Whittaker's
    old spectacles, smudges to be spat and
    polished with old salts...
    So it's none of anyone's child of sorrow
    of anyone's lookout ribbon.
    Eliza White, blue at the mizzen,
    at the flap of a bonnet.
    Eliza White. Someone still standing.

Andrew Motion & The British Library Archive

In the Stacks

The Archives at the British Library hold manuscripts relating to major British writers in poetry, prose and drama, on paper, vellum and electronic media.

The Library's modern historical collections include material on the royal household, leading statesmen, diplomats, colonial governors and other civil and military office-holders. They also comprise material relating to individuals with significant roles in public life, including reformers, journalists, and public campaigners. Significant also are the archives of scientists, mathematicians, and medical researchers.

The Library's extensive sound and moving image collections include live recordings of theatre (both established like the Royal Shakespeare Company, and experimental), poetry and prose, plus broadcast radio and TV programmes, including the BBC's radio archive. Our oral history collection (audio and videotape) covers many subject areas such as British colonialism, religion, the history of medicine, industry, politics, the arts, women's history and Jewish history. The British Library is also home to the Newspaper Archive and the UK Web Archive.

Rachel Foss
Lead Curator, Modern Literary Manuscripts

Officially I had carte blanche to look anywhere in the British Library for my subject(s) for this commission. In fact when I reported for duty Rachel Foss, knowing my interest in writing of and about the First World War, had already looked out various items that she thought might spark my imagination. The manuscripts of Wilfred Owen's poems, for instance; and a letter to Rupert Brooke's girlfriend Cathleen Nesbitt, sent by one of the friends who buried him on the island of Skyros (and enclosing some leaves from the olive tree that bends over his grave); and some censored letters sent by Indian troops serving with the British Army. All these were indeed very suggestive things, and all of them made me want to write about them. But so too was a less 'written' series of documents - the collected accounts by school children of seeing a zeppelin over London - and one thing that had nothing to do with writing at all. A photograph of a soldier washing in a rain-filled shell crater: an immediately touching and compelling image. Taken all together, these things have made the whole experience of delving into the archives at once salutary and bracing for me. Because I have seen glimpses of the living past, and been allowed to bring it back above ground again into the light.

Andrew Motion

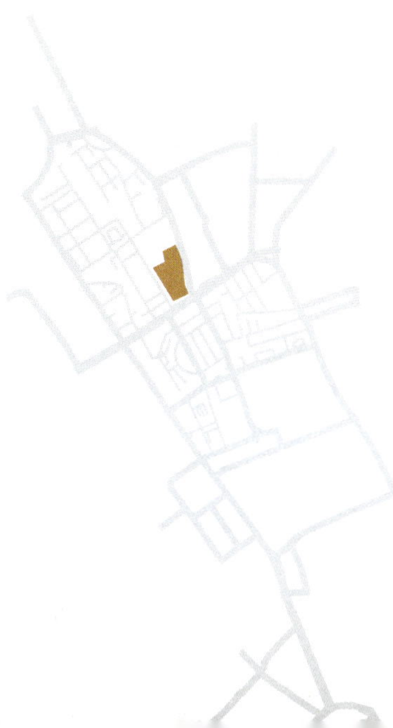

1.

These dry scraps are five olive leaves
Denis Browne pulled from the olive tree
growing over the grave he had just dug

for his friend Rupert Brooke in 1915
and posted back to Cathleen Nesbitt.
They look as brittle and delicate now

as the scales of a surprisingly large fish,
but I think they are what it says they are,
because strange as it might seem I stood

myself under the same tree 50 years later,
aged 17 and so beginning to work out how
my life might be measured and must end

thanks in part to the procession of red ants
marching from a narrow crack in the coping
designed for the grave by Brooke's mother

after Denis Browne and his funeral party
had made their farewell and left the island,
sailing towards his own death in Gallipoli.

2.

In their trench now but these same soldiers
with their soft caps and kilts, their bare knees
and open wind-nipped faces, will all disappear

over the top in a moment and so leave behind
the terrier, the jaunty white terrier called Argos
who, if one of them returns, will raise his head

because this man smells like the same master
that set out all those years ago, although to see
the changes in him now no one would think so.

3.

What flew in from another land
filled up the sky above the Strand –

an insect like a huge cigar
splashed about with tongues of fire

and someone crouching at a door
despite our guns' tremendous roar

to drop his load of shiny bombs
across our dark and quiet homes.

Remember, I was still a child
and never thought I might be killed.

I liked the bombs, I liked the fire,
I liked the huge high-up cigar,

I liked especially how our lights
cut misty pathways through the night

and how my footsteps made no sound
when I walked there not on the ground.

4.

This report is a continuation of one numbered 303A and relates to the fortnight concluded on 13th inst., which contains a selection of extracts from Indian letters. These cited here illustrate how almost impossible it is for Oriental correspondence to be effective as a barrier.

Among signal orchestrations to show courage and duty Orientals excel in the art of conveying their information without saying anything definite (*words missing here*). When they have meaning to convey they are apt to use a phrase such as 'Think it over until you understand it', or some equivalent. It naturally follows that their news is exceedingly vague and will give rise to wild rumours.

It has nevertheless been possible to draw some conclusions; eg: the prospect of a return to the firing line appears to be regarded with something approaching (*word missing here*), as in: 'My brother, this is no war. It is the final destruction of the world. A whole world is being killed. If I ever return I shall tell you very much. If I end here, what is there to tell.'

In the same way, extracts show the man who has served and been wounded feels he has amply fulfilled his obligation, as in: 'The guns are firing. The Kings are looking on. Like dust the dead are lying before the trench. Thus are we sacrificed.'

5.

What tree was felled in what remote forest,
then dragged by what engine or elephant
through what jungle to what paper-mill
in what sea-port, then shipped to what dock

then sold how and cut how and bought how
for this particular man on this particular day
in Craiglockhart War Hospital in Edinburgh
to single it out thinking, Now, here, with this

pen on this table-top with this my right hand
I shall write down these words in this order
to catch what I am trying to say then pass it
along the corridor to him who just happens

to be recovering there from his own troubles,
and who, when not practicing his golf swing,
will read them and recommend that one thing
becomes another, for example the word 'dead',

which he thinks should be 'doomed', and also
that 'silent minds' be changed to 'patient minds'.

6.

Eventually, at the very end of everything, the last man
emerges through trees without any leaves or branches
and comes to a halt on the greasy slope of a bomb-crater

where in a brown puddle he sees his own face looking up
to remind him of the need to wash himself. Laying aside
on the pitted bank his tin hat and satchel, his lousy jacket,

he inches forward as close as he dare to the water's edge
where mud immediately swallows his boots to the ankle,
spreads his legs while at the same time leaning forward

as if the air itself were solid enough to stop him toppling,
and scoops a dark handful from the pool. The impression,
as he uses his left hand to smear the water over his neck

and jaw, and his right to continue the process over his chin
and mouth, is of a man taking a firm grip on his own face
before twisting his head off the delicate screw of his neck

and rather than washing himself throwing away his skull
along with everything inside it that can never be forgotten
and in this way, at the very end of everything, be clean again.

Mario Petrucci & The Royal College of Surgeons of England

The Bone Ship

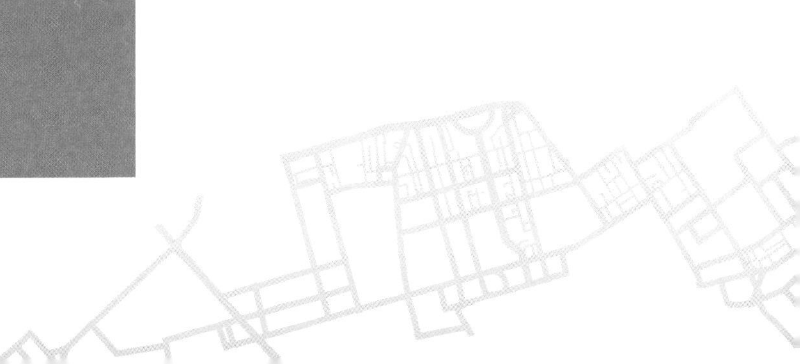

The Royal College of Surgeons' Archives contain the records of the College's activities from 1800 to the present day, and of the College's predecessor the Company of Surgeons, 1745-1800.

The archives also hold a diverse range of other archive and manuscript collections relating to medicine and surgery from the 16th to the 20th century. We hold the professional and personal papers of eminent surgeons including John Hunter, Astley Paston Cooper, Joseph Lister and Berkeley Moynihan. We now have the First World War British and New Zealand patient files of pioneering plastic surgeon Sir Harold Gillies.

There are also a variety of individual items including diaries, photograph albums, lecture notes, drawings and even recipe books! The archives also hold many unexpected items relating to medicine, surgery, natural history and anatomy including: a diary kept by a Resurrectionist (grave robber); sketches of the "heads of murderers" whose bodies were dissected at the College in the 19th century; and illustrated letters to Rudyard Kipling from his relation Edward Burne-Jones.

Louise King
Archivist

IN
ROYAL COLLEGE OF SURGE
OF ENGLAND

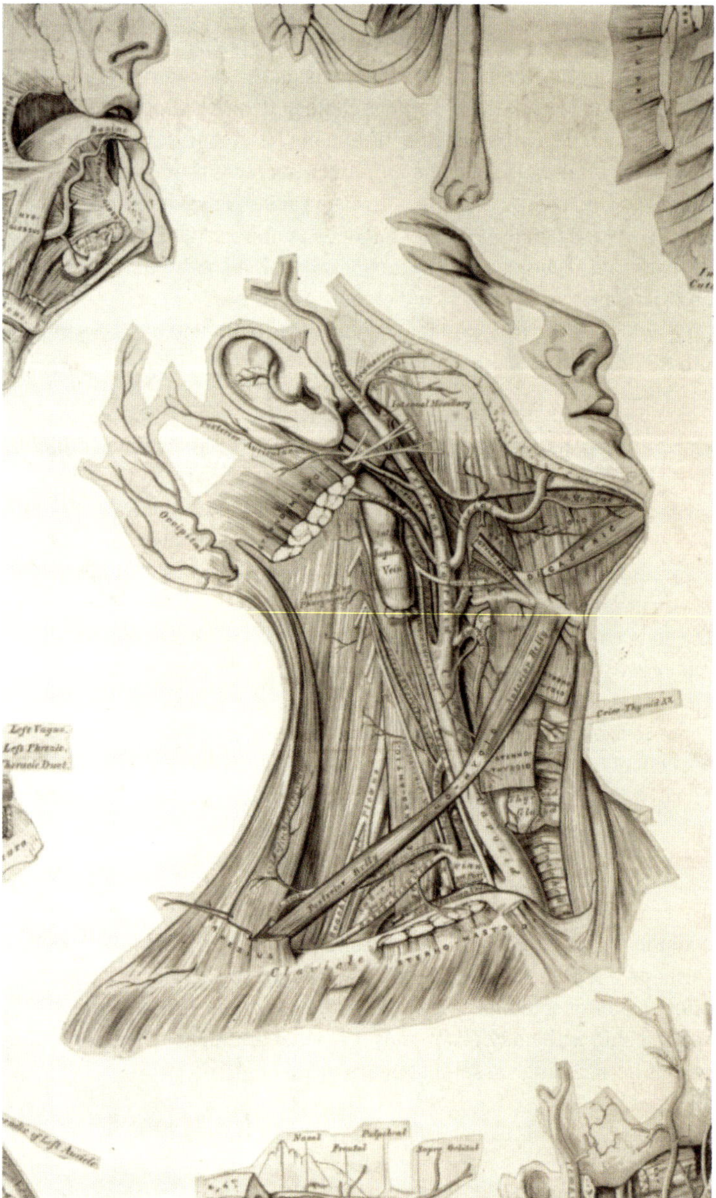
Occipital
Posterior Auricular
Internal Maxillary
Crico-Thyroid Art.
Left Vagus.
Left Phrenic.
Thoracic Duct.
Clavicle
Posterior Belly
Anterior Belly
Nasal
Frontal
Palpebral
Supra Orbital

The Bone Ship bears manifold cargo from the archives of the Royal College of Surgeons of England. These eleven poems address: war wounds, and WWI facial reconstructions; cutting-edge surgical methodologies; historical attitudes to flesh (which almost invariably implicate gender); John Hunter (the Isaac Newton of surgery) and his nerve-jangling tooth transplants; the archives themselves; the Blitz (the College was hit) through a surrealist lens; venereal disease among British troops in India, and body snatching, both rendered provocatively though a 'cut-up' approach; ruined body parts presented as haiku, as if each were a kind of materialist, surgical chakra; and, not least, the irrepressible strangeness of human anatomy, its inherent beauty, even in pathology.

Much of the archive material I studied drew a deeply complex, visceral response. The writing followed, stitching along those difficult lines, seeking to stabilise a body of work that might be challenging, vivid and unflinching – though always, in some essential way, humane. *The Bone Ship* sails in the conviction that modern poetry can be clear and resonant in its *sound* – in its 'textual music' – without being linear or prosaically paraphrasable; that words can be very much at the centre of our experience of words; and that poems can unfold to *enact* consciousness rather than merely provide commentary upon it. Language as a medium utterly involved in the processes it explores seems essential, to me, whether one is delving into the 'ontological' aspects of medical science or the poignancy of bodily suffering. Moreover, our seemingly inexhaustible appetite for 'progress' casts long, collective shadows. I can't unravel these alone. I invite the reader into the text as co-creator, in dialogue with its meaning.

Those porous membranes between poetry and science, especially the evolution of medical insight and practice, have long fascinated me. Perhaps *The Bone Ship* will help to show how the history of surgery offers a post-mortem (or even some kind of prognosis?) on society's relationship with body. If not, may it at least give pause to reflect anew on this astonishing vessel that bears us through life.

Mario Petrucci

Bullets

Palpate for a thrill.
With stethoscope hear the bruit.
Exert your will. Cope with the wide-open fruit.

All clothing – removed. Once they would tidy each
wound unwisely as if its inside-out pastry
were there to be trimmed.

Excise what is purply
or black. Is your victim slack or stable?
Resist any unfresh scalpel. A full-thickness puncture must

mesh in layers – imagine stitching ragged lasagne. I insist
holes in the face be closed loosely. Brace
yourself for TV shows

that slice it out
crudely when blink or cough can kill.
There's every chance it will be walled off – shunned

by the cunning body. Or it will toil to the surface
slowly: as with fleshless smile the fallen
have done

in the fertile soils of France.

Surgical love

They had to enucleate both
my eyes. Yet your shape snakes
bright in that cinema sightlessness makes.

My wasted belly – opened exploratorily
to a stewful of eels. They writhe
still for a taste of you.

As tinned copper wire
snipped from its sheath: calves stripped
of inflammatory nerve. But toe-tips remember

your tight-woven wreath. Thumbs. Fingers. Elbow
and wrist. All gangrenous – gone. Slow
ghost-hands reach for your waist.

This breast dissected
to beached ribs. My bone ship.
Heart bails alone for you its last salt heat.

Lip and palate. Tongue and chin. Sigh and whisper
uninstilled. Yet the will immaterial
slips within.

Hip and thigh.
That softer flesh. To cinerator.
Crematorium. Dust and ash. And oh

in their jars these parts so prolonged. But
the sum shall throng in you
wherever you are.

Methods

We relieve now with lasers:
those potent beams never to look at
except side-on. But have we ever believed

whatever can be seen can't cut?
Or vaporize. Malign cells that fraternize
to dominance in cervix, larynx, skin. Photoablation

blasts in to dissolve all bonds:
resolves tumoured windpipes, plasma
-plumes eyes without sensation, reminds of glows shed

ripe-hot from noses of re-
entrant craft. Liquid nitrogen fumes.
Feel that firming shiver and kill: frostbite's wolf rebred

to steaming husky for
liver and penis – pulling death's
bright sled south through teeming obfusc. In mouth

or epidermis: high
frequency current. Eyes
warrant see-through shavings, sliver by sliver.

Laparoscopy
for hernia, gall bladder, cyst. No
need to lift the bonnet for cancerous colon, prostate,

uterus: soon the risk
-reducing robot will drive. Save that
CyberKnife for loaf - neck - spine. Wait till *ultra* or

nano bloom wrong cells to
micro-carnations. Kneel or recline
for tests that long to bless – what in moderation

we tolerate must heal in excess.

10 5 '41

Royal College of Surgeons Hunterian Museum

night's trap
door flung down – loosing
lung & liver slack in jars & Hunter's animal

catch caught up in preservation now finds itself
in War dropping unresembling jaws
at the roof-

entering photo
-flash that disinters femur from its
human frame to rashly reassemble it with elk: a mixed &

mixing Last Trump as all through London Lucifer's black-
winged angel hails its Germanic stac-
-cato load to

make this
Golem of many heads & tails
from pickled or desiccated flesh whose wrecking swelling

boil of flame bursts dead fauna forward under fire in red
-white sheets to resurrect through
the galleries

down the streets
Blighty's Old dead & her
Fresh whose digits touch their fleshless tips mid-

air – who clutch at flight curling lips in
hissing heat too brief to
kiss

18th century surgeon John Hunter transplanted a human tooth into the comb of a cockerel (item P 56, Hunterian Museum). He later attempted tooth transplants between humans. Young female donors were preferred.

P 56

In flesh borders he gardens
knowledge. Sinks it there as if a tulip bulb

jaundiced in bloody turf. In the tiny heat of this
flushed terrain what will grow its

one ice flower? For weeks cockerel
wakes dentine & pulp with gargling yells of yellow-

toothed migraine. Outside queue the sick unfed to sell
live canine & incisor. In young skulls

each small resistance to his pliers grips
bonily a bloody instant – then slides. Did those jelly-blood

teeth in their leather-red comb dryly pliantly rough to touch
wobble with undervalued pain as much as

the congealed curls of these girls unhealed?
In Hunter's Museum in forensic section I gawp at how close

is cockerel crop to pickled-walnut brain. His upright fang
whiffs modernity's note of raised brow:

Bizarre. Unusual. Is this in faint that
same tainted track thought would take to Auschwitz

in crammed trucks of curiosity – a world where
even innocent dentures piled versus

toothlessness betray blind mind grinding
to its ruthless point?

Gillies

Plastic surgeon (1882 – 1960)

I advance flaps – loop tubes of skin
: tunnels
to transport cellular troops to required fronts

A blunt nose might begin near the collar – a brow
above the ear
– a palate reach up from neck – so each may attempt

the smile for the wife : as with that luckless gunner from
HMS *Warspite*
now wearing goggles of his own chest as though at dinner

he had lifted to the blenched & boggling face a tucked-in
napkin of himself
Ah – they have said how my knife this sculpting scalpel

is war's angel that accosts flesh to make bridgeheads
of itself : but I
never ask whether those features remember their

once-entrenched strips of body : the man bled
of expression
waking to such lost manoeuvres of lips –

feeling all across that leathered mask
every
where a woman's hand touched

Chief sources: 'Plastic Surgery of the Face' (H.D. Gillies: London, 1920) + Gillies British patient files [RCSEng Archives catalogue ref. MS0513/1/1].

Resurrection Man

Joseph Naples: body snatcher

Saturday –
At night went out & got 3.
Sold to Mr. Cline St. Thomas's.

Sunday –
Looked to see what funerals were about.
At Home all night.

Monday –
Got paid for the 3 adults & settled.
Met & settled with Mordecei. At Home all night.
Miss Naples.

Tuesday –
Brought the Shovils from Bartholomew. The dogs
flew at us. Could not succeed. Met early
at Mr. Vickers. Came Home
intoxsicated.

Wednesday –
At night went out & got 10 whole. Opened another
whole though bad with the small pox. Found
a watch planted.

Thursday –
Went to Pancrass. Got 2. 1 adult 1 small.
Went to Bunhill Row got 6. 1 with the throat cut.
Sold the extremities.

Friday –
The moon at the full.
Could not go got Drunk. Slept a sleep
of the unburied. I did not do
Anything.

Chief sources: Joseph Naples [RCSEng Archives catalogue ref. MS0024] + 'The Diary of a Resurrectionist, 1811-1812' (James Blake Bailey: London, 1896).

Wound

(1914 – 1918)

Exposed at a brow
that humming bonnet of bone

Inflammation as lipsticked mouths
pouting through colon

How the bullet before it
comes to rest can random-walk anatomy

Lung as a scarlet deep-sea
squid curling its fork of new-found tongue

Alive and liverish through
its chest – that layered slot private as a girl's

The shot-through organs in their necrotic nest
rounded to misshapen eggs

Wrist or leg as clotted wood shrapnel-knobbed
A tin helmet that couldn't

save studded with fist-sized cloves: those pot
-holing caves in brain-

flecked skull – Neck
parted to second grin – Face squirmed

too big too open
to a coal-black lily – A single

wormhole
tidily through its blue

& fig
-slack heart

Chief source: A. Kirkpatrick Maxwell
[RCSEng Archives catalogue ref. MS0023/1].

Lords

(House of Lords Speech: 17 May 1897)

There is no more difficult thing for a surgeon
than to give advice to a man when it is
safe for him to enter when he has
contracted syphilis.

In the early stages there is no general effect upon
the system. The mere fact of prostitution
affords reasonable probability.

If any woman chooses a position a magistrate must
be satisfied. One matter which I
did not like: the woman

pronounced clear received a certificate. Chaplains
attend the women. On all hands that
savours pretty strongly –

I have been informed on credible testimony it was
not a rare thing for them to be restored.
How wholesome

a moral influence hospital exerts upon the lower
classes. A severe accident might be
a blessing.

Objection? The women are humbled while nothing
is done to deal with the men? I confess
that seems a sentimental one.

Periodic inspection? Let it be done not in a sort of parade – but let every soldier be introduced solemnly.

Failure. I trust that this House will give distinct encouragement to India in the good
and Christian course.
Cheers.

Sole source: 'British Troops In India (Health). Speech by Lord Lister on Monday, 17th May 1897.' [RCSEng Archives catalogue ref. MS0021/7/26, Joseph Lister Papers].

Pathological Haiku

testis – blushed
plump apple thrush started
but could not finish

*

womb – become
blue-veined skull eyelessly
bowed in study

*

curl of colon –
broken-off coral curved
with polyps

*

ulcerated kidney :
encrusted caverns linked greyly
through pink karst

*

halved stomach : smooth with
black sheen as though
avocado stone had been

*

martian
liver – becoined
with lichen

*

woman – from under
one breast : mottled garland
of rust carnations

*

tongue
hung wordless in swill –
empurpled eel

*

eye –
grey olive
pupil-pitted

*

skull –
bleached oak of bone
grown from one socket

*

farthing hole in
heart's rare gourd – that
single round of love

Sole source: Astley Paston Cooper, 'Pathological Drawings' [RCSEng Archives catalogue ref. MS0008/4/5].

Archive

for The Royal College of Surgeons of England

how
many tomes how
many

times
must eye & hand caress
flesh on

paper
unzipping undressing in ink
or water

-colour
before they are satisfied? – those
early surgeons

in love with
anatomy before the body became this
marriage for the sake

of the children
where eyes meet across the table & hands
reach then fingers stretch

only to pass that
scalpel – though there is something vital here
some future unbreakable

written & drawn in
cut & suture on these old pages put immaculately
to bed – this care to hold

open a door to let
sight maybe a life walk cleanly intimately through
: thus shall body with

surgeon stutter *I*
do rightfully shakingly nuptial forever husband
with wife unless

that mistress
or master – the patient – so achingly kept
anaesthetised

& too long
under the knife nevertheless
wakes up

Fiona
Sampson
&
Tower Hamlets
Local History
Library and
Archives

Paradise Row

Tower Hamlets Local History Library and Archives is an unparalleled resource for the social and political history of the East End during its urbanisation, development and redevelopment over three centuries.

There are over 10,000 title deeds recording the transfer of properties, the earliest of which dates back to 1384. We also hold archives from individuals, businesses, groups and organisations. For example, we hold the papers of Edith Ramsay (1895-1983), educationalist and social campaigner which reveal fascinating details of Stepney's red light district in the 1950s and the embryonic Black community in parts of Whitechapel, and the records of the St George's German Lutheran Church which demonstrate the extent of the often-overlooked German population in east London. Records of the East End Dwellings Company chart early attempts to deal with the area's notorious housing problems.

We have a growing collection of oral histories such as those of Bangladeshi residents who engaged in housing activism and anti-racist community work during the 1970s-1980s; Somali seamen who settled in the borough from the 1960s; contemporary African-Caribbean, Somali and Bangladeshi women residents; and older residents of Old Ford and Fish Island, industrial areas adjacent to the new Olympic Park.

Tamsin Bookey
Heritage Manager

Tower Hamlets Council
Building a great place to live, work and play
Tower Hamlets Local History
Library & Archives

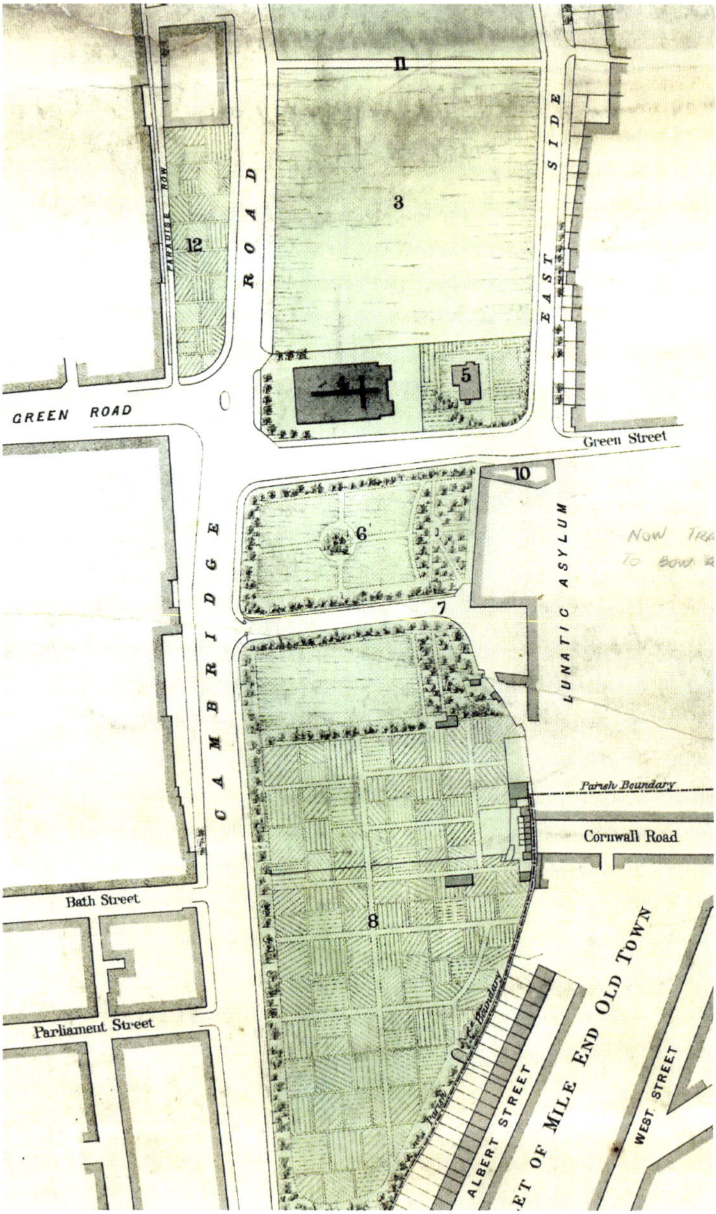
11
3
EAST SIDE
ROAD
PARADISE ROW
12
5
GREEN ROAD
Green Street
10
LUNATIC ASYLUM
6
CAMBRIDGE
7
Parish Boundary
Cornwall Road
Bath Street
8
Parliament Street
Parish Boundary
ALBERT STREET
ET OF MILE END OLD TOWN
WEST STREET

I've always loved the way Tower Hamlets has been shaped by successive waves of immigration, some of them within my own family. But polemic, however sincere, isn't poetry. So these poems are all set in the domestic, private sphere: in the heart of the lives people make for themselves, among those routines and odd moments that are individuals' own. They're snapshots, fragments of lives.

All their narrators are women and children (I imagine Micah as a late teenager). Since I'm a poet and not an archivist, I've dramatized the way succeeding lives are lived in the very same streets and houses by setting each of my scenes exactly twenty years apart. Not all my characters are immigrants, but they're all members of communities who have settled in Tower Hamlets. I chose not to patronize them by using broken English. These inner lives are fluent, whatever language they're being thought in.

I picked Paradise Row, a real street, because of the symbolic hopefulness of its name, and because the houses have the right kind of history. They escaped the Blitz (I wanted Sidney to be safe in his childhood home, having returned from evacuation as many children did, not only after the Phoney War but also later: my mother among them). These houses also have a pattern of multiple occupancy, both recently and back into the nineteenth century.

I hope that my characters' names and what we catch them thinking speak for themselves, telling us about the communities they belong to and, a little, how they live. They are: Irish washer-girl, a Jewish teenager whose family work in a sewing sweat-shop, a surviving member of the area's Huguenot community, two kids, someone who is home-sick for the Caribbean, someone else who is still traumatised by his journey to the UK, and an observant Muslim home-maker.

Fiona Sampson

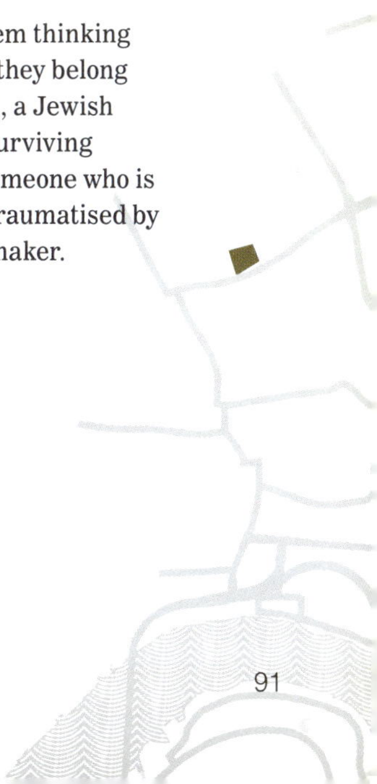

Washday

1864: Lily

Warmth and wet
rising in clouds from clean sheets –
everything lifted

as if on hoists
into the new
smell of wetness.

I will swim down to the river
arm over arm among sheets
clouds and pearled river lights.

Singer

1884: Micah

Under your tongue
a sewing machine jabbers
takka-takka
where the root gleams
like a needle.

Night and day
your tongue ties me up
mother – thread
drawn tight
like kisses and curses.

Tea-Service

1904: Lenny

The Indian Tree
is pink and blue.
Tongues of leaf

shoot up like flames.
The Indian Tree's
a burning bush,

its tendrils curl along
the cup's bare skin
like a tattoo.

In Gramma's hand
the skinny cup floats –
a milky disc

a scrying lens
and her one yellow eye
floats above it,

a blob of cream
the cat could lick lick lick
clean out of its socket.

Doorstep

1924: Genevieve

Our doorstep shines
where the wet gathers.
This fallen world is grey

except for rain's
unexpected
grace
            rinsing the air
street
and neighbourhood

pouring us
from ourselves
into ourselves –

Condiments

1944: Sidney

The salt and pepper
are on the table.
The child sees
two soldiers –

they stand
to attention
on orange
seersucker.

Suppertime voices and Ovaltine
fill the boy
until he yawns.
Comfort and victory –

brightly
the short salt
and tall pepper
wink in lamplight.

Fish Stew

1964: Evangeline

Cracklebone!
A carcass flips
along the drainer

its black meat full
of a stew
of dock water.

Slip your hand
into this
decay

this slithery undoing.
The pan
makes a mirror

holding up
your face.
One glaucous eye

stares back at you
out of ruin.

Double-Glazing

1984: Safraz

The double-glazing
shakes
as lorries pass.

Sometimes I feel
it chattering
down my nerves

sometimes
all around me like
a frightened heart.

Sometimes I dream
the motor of the ferry's
shaking loose

and I'm trapped between decks.
Stink of diesel, slop
of storm water...

Coffee

2004: Hiba

A brown disc
slops at its
own brim.

Coffee occludes itself
and milk
occludes it.

Milk in the children's
coffee,
almond biscuits

on a tray
at four
just how their father likes.

His smile
flutters
around my ankles

the way light flutters
on the kitchen
floor.

Images

cover page: Great St. Helen's, Bishopsgate Street, 1880. Credit: the British Library.

page 7: Photograph of Imtiaz Dharker. Credit: Ayesha Dharker Taylor

page 9: Photograph of Saint Paul's Cathedral; source: http://commons.wikimedia.org/wiki/File:St._Paul%27s_Cathedral,_London.JPG; user: Eluveitie; image modified to greyscale.

page 10: Photograph of bomb-damaged Bodley-Garner High Altar, c. 1940. In the foreground can be seen two putti ('cherub') figures, previously part of the altar table. Credit: The Architectural of St Paul's Cathedral.

page 23: Photograph of David Harsent. Credit: Simon Harsent.

page 25: Photograph of Freemasons' Hall; source: http://commons.wikimedia.org/wiki/File:Freemasons%27_Hall,_London.JPG; user: Eluveitie; image modified to greyscale.

page 26: The jazz musician and singer, Louis Armstrong, revealed an aspiration to join freemasonry by becoming a member of the American fraternal organisation, the Knights of Pythias. The Knights often had brass bands which may have attracted Armstrong and other musicians. Credit: The Archives of the Library and Museum of Freemasonry.

page 39: Photograph of Hackney Archives. Credit: Carmela Pietrangelo; image modified to greyscale.

page 40: Manor House in Dalston Lane where the Refuge for the Destitute was based during the time when the minutes that Simon looked at were being created. Credit: Hackney Archives.

page 53: Photograph of Andrew Motion. Credit: Johnny Ring.

page 55: Photograph of the British Library. Credit: Paul Grundy; image modified and set to greyscale.

page 56: Photograph showing a group of Highland Territorial soldiers in a trench, armed with bayonets. Several of them are wearing kilts, which was the uniform for some of the Scottish battalions that fought in the First World War. Also in the trench we can see a small dog: many battalions had dogs as mascots. Credit: British Library.

page 67: Photograph of The Royal College of Surgeons, from http://commons.wikimedia.org/wiki/File:Royal_College_of_Surgeons_of_England_1.jpg; user: Jbarta; image modified to greyscale.

page 68: MS0346, India Proofs for Anatomy, Descriptive and Surgical (Gray's Anatomy) 1858. Credit: The Royal College of Surgeons' Archives.

page 87: Photograph of Fiona Sampson. Credit: Mark Bassett

page 89: Photograph of Tower Hamlets Archives. Credit: Carmela Pietrangelo; image modified to greyscale.

page 90: Section from a Plan of the Poor's Lands in the Parish of St Matthew, Bethnal Green, 1868.

The Architectural Archive of St Paul's Cathedral
www.stpauls.co.uk/Cathedral-History/The-Collections

The Archives of the Library and Museum of Freemasonry
www.freemasonry.london.museum/catalogue

Hackney Archives
www.hackney.gov.uk/ca-archives

Archives at the British Library
www.bl.uk

The Royal College of Surgeons' Archives
www.rcseng.ac.uk/museums/archives

Tower Hamlets Local History Library and Archives
www.ideastore.co.uk/local-history